Energetic Questions

Life's Simple Answers

Fred Shadian

Energetic Questions

Life's Simple Answers

Energetic: Active transformation
Questions: To elicit information
Energetic Questions:
Active transformation to elicit information.

"This book can potentially guide you to answer your deepest, inquisitive questions about life and the meaning of your life."

Fred Shadian

Inspired by

Yasū' al-Masih
(Jesus, the Anointed One)

Gibran Kahlil Gibran

Saint Francis of Assisi

O'Sensei Morihei Ueshiba

Professor David John Harris

Grandmaster Fook Yeung

Grandmaster Choa Kok Sui

In chronological order of inspiration

A special thank you to the kindred spirits, who walked
upon my path and continue to walk beside me.
As we walk on this earth together.

A Big Thank You & Acknowledgment:

Below is the list of the people that supported the printing campaign of this book via crowd founding efforts to print 1000 Books to Give to 1000 People.

Paulo Agelidis, Sandeep Aggarwal, Cecilia Bax,
Leonard Benoit, Anthony Beyrouti,
John & Monica Blackhall, Michele Buchignani,
Tony Cass, Nigel Cook, Daber Family (Damien, Esther,
Hanna, Hanny, Horst, Jim, John, Marla, Milan, Ruth,
Tanja, Tobias, Zora), Margo Daoud,
Jeff Guy Debou, Andrew Elizaga, Jenica Geisler,
Shane Gibson, Angie & Bernd Giese,
Anthony Guidera, Louis Hajjar, Joel M Harris,
Marcia Harter, Christie, Ethan & Doug Hess,
Teal Hodgson, Federico J. Ituarte, Kolbrun Kjerulf,
Jesse Knotts, Charelton Kubera, Brian Ludwig,
Jonathan Lusk, Greg MacChesney, Nick Marinos,
Dawna Masters, Chantelle & Lee Middleton,
Stuart Anthony Morse, Gina A Nolan,
Eden and Daniel O'Hara, Debbie Ottenbreit,
Dru Overwijk, Mark Pace, Hew Padmore,
Jini Pillai & Louie Pinto, John Podgorny,
Karen Rauch Carter, Linda Romeril, Nelson Salahub,
Keith W Salustro, Scott Sargeant,
Chantal Sejourne-Daitch, Elizabeth Serrick,
Abed Shadian, Isaac A Shadian,
Jibran Marsden-Shadian, Fred Scott, Lillian Tong,
Derek GC White, Gary Soghomonian, Laura Smith,
Peter & Donna Stolting, Gregg Turner,
LLoyd Verberg, John Vergara, Pete Vanderley,
Barb Vargo, Holly Walen, Rick Worrall,
Kate Vigneault & Ron Wilson, Kelly S. Worden.

Inspired by

Yasū' al-Masih
(Jesus, the Anointed One)

Gibran Kahlil Gibran

Saint Francis of Assisi

O'Sensei Morihei Ueshiba

Professor David John Harris

Grandmaster Fook Yeung

Grandmaster Choa Kok Sui

In chronological order of inspiration

A special thank you to the kindred spirits, who walked
upon my path and continue to walk beside me.
As we walk on this earth together.

A Big Thank You & Acknowledgment:

Below is the list of the people that supported the printing campaign of this book via crowd founding efforts to print 1000 Books to Give to 1000 People.

Paulo Agelidis, Sandeep Aggarwal, Cecilia Bax, Leonard Benoit, Anthony Beyrouti, John & Monica Blackhall, Michele Buchignani, Tony Cass, Nigel Cook, Daber Family (Damien, Esther, Hanna, Hanny, Horst, Jim, John, Marla, Milan, Ruth, Tanja, Tobias, Zora), Margo Daoud, Jeff Guy Debou, Andrew Elizaga, Jenica Geisler, Shane Gibson, Angie & Bernd Giese, Anthony Guidera, Louis Hajjar, Joel M Harris, Marcia Harter, Christie, Ethan & Doug Hess, Teal Hodgson, Federico J. Ituarte, Kolbrun Kjerulf, Jesse Knotts, Charelton Kubera, Brian Ludwig, Jonathan Lusk, Greg MacChesney, Nick Marinos, Dawna Masters, Chantelle & Lee Middleton, Stuart Anthony Morse, Gina A Nolan, Eden and Daniel O'Hara, Debbie Ottenbreit, Dru Overwijk, Mark Pace, Hew Padmore, Jini Pillai & Louie Pinto, John Podgorny, Karen Rauch Carter, Linda Romeril, Nelson Salahub, Keith W Salustro, Scott Sargeant, Chantal Sejourne-Daitch, Elizabeth Serrick, Abed Shadian, Isaac A Shadian, Jibran Marsden-Shadian, Fred Scott, Lillian Tong, Derek GC White, Gary Soghomonian, Laura Smith, Peter & Donna Stolting, Gregg Turner, LLoyd Verberg, John Vergara, Pete Vanderley, Barb Vargo, Holly Walen, Rick Worrall, Kate Vigneault & Ron Wilson, Kelly S. Worden.

Dedication:
To the generous heart of Joseph E. Beyrouti.
May your smiling spirit continue to bless us.

Gratitude:
To my beloved wife Ruth Daber-Shadian for making this book a reality, the countless hours of feedback, editing and wonderful graphics and illustrations for the book.

Thank you to my Family for all their Support:
To my wonderful parents Camilla & Yacoub and
Abed, Anthony, Bassem, Billy, Camilla, Carol, Charbel, Deana, Ellias, Francois, Gaby, George, Ghassan, Jack, Jamal, Jessica, Jibran, Joseph, Josephine, Julian, Michel, Kay, Louis, Maggie, Margo, Safwat, Salemah, Shafia.

Special Thanks to:
Dr. Stewart Blaikie for his body alignment wisdom.
Tony Cass for applying these principles in healing.
Deana Daoud for editing and proofreading the book.
Lila Elliott for her continuous friendship and support.
Shane Gibson for applying the principles in business.
Angi & Bernd Giese for the use of their retreat.
Jesse Knotts for applying these principles in golf.
Brian Ludwig for encouraging me to keep writing.
Maureen Freeman for encouraging me to tune in.
Greg MacChesney for applying these principles in life.
Nick Marinos for applying these principles in movies.
Jibran Marsden-Shadian for cover design feedback.
Mark Pace for the continuous encouragement.
Hew Padmore for applying these principles in teaching.
Susanna Puppato for sharing the teachings.
Elizabeth Serrick for early editing and feedback.
Pete Vanderley for applying these principles in teaching.

Energetic Questions Contents

The Beginning

On a stormy, snowy winter day in 1997, I was at home meditating in my living room, enjoying the weather elements at play. At the end of my meditation, I began to feel the room getting warmer. I looked out the window and noticed glorious sun rays bursting through the clouds, creating a glistening sparkle of light on the snow. It was breathtakingly beautiful.

Knowing how powerful the energy of the five elements is, I decided that it would be a perfect time to walk up the summit behind the house to do a meditation. The plateau on top of the hill provided all five elements in one location. I noticed the Earth, Water, Fire, Wind and Space surrounding me. In this wide open space, you could see for miles, overlooking surrounding areas. It truly felt as though I was on top of the world.

A gentle wind was blowing through the trees and the air smelled fresh, crisp and clean. You could almost see the ions dancing in the air. With every breath I took, I felt an expansion in my energy body. As I exhaled, I could feel stored up tension release from my physical and emotional body.

Looking over the snow covered branches of the nearby Garry Oaks, I noticed the snow was melting into water crystals that were glittering with rainbow sparkles.

The energy from the sun was warming up every cell in my body. I could see the heat rise from the trees as I watched in awe how the melting snow swirled into a ring around the trunk of the tree. It was a magnificent sight.

While experiencing the beauty of the five elements,
I walked toward my normal meditation spot to practice
my Energetic Chi Kung. I felt a sense of being
completely grounded on top of the summit.

I began my rhythmic breathing that is known as;

Energetic Breathing 3, 1, 3, 1
Inhale for 3 seconds, Hold for 1.
Exhale for 3 seconds, Hold for 1.
Repeat for 9 full cycles.
(Smile as you practice this exercise).

While standing in my meditation stance, I was slowly
breathing in and out this energetic experience allowing
the Sun to bless me with its glory. Feeling the radiant
solar energy flowing through my crown and third eye
chakra. The energy kept flowing through my whole
body. At the same time, I could feel my foot chakras
rooting and the base of my spine grounding into the
Earth. In my mind's eye, I could see beams of light
spreading underneath the ground.
The solar energy filled my whole body with energetic
light, love, peace and harmony.
For the first time I could feel my energy body and my
physical body become one. As I continued to meditate,
I felt the presence of an energy being in front of me.

I slowly opened my eyes and saw...

O'Sensei Morihei Ueshiba, the founder of Aikido, was standing about 20 feet in front of me. I wondered if I was hallucinating, or if he was really there with me.

His philosophy of AiKiDo (Harmony, Energy, Way) had always inspired me to look at martial arts as a way of life and impacted the way I teach and think.

Doubt and fear came over me, followed by peaceful joy that encouraged me to experience the bliss of his energetic presence right in front of me.

I closed my eyes to ground myself and to be certain, that this was real. As I opened my eyes again, I saw that he was standing in the same spot, blessing me with his profound wisdom.

As I continued to enjoy the bliss, I could feel my meridians and chakras opening up. I took a couple of steps toward him. As I got closer to him, he disappeared. I continued to walk towards the spot where he had stood. I felt another blissful wave of energy.

I turned around and saw that he now was standing where I had been meditating.

A joyous feeling of oneness came over me.

I was thinking out loud,

"This old man is as tricky as ever."

O'Sensei is well known for vanishing from his attackers, just to be found standing right behind them.

Again my mind was going a hundred miles per hour, wondering if this visitation was real or not.

I walked back to my meditation spot, where he was standing. As I approached, he again disappeared, and then reappeared at the original spot.

As I got back to my meditation location, I closed my eyes and enjoyed this wonderful energetic experience of witnessing O'Sensei appear, disappear, and reappear.

I said to myself, "Whether this is real or not, it does not matter. What really matters is the feelings that I am experiencing right now. The blissful joy was buzzing through my whole body."

As I stood there and grounded myself into this energetic bliss, I said a little prayer asking for energetic protection and guidance.
A stream of consciousness thought came through me. The message kept repeating, over and over again.
I walked back to the house, grabbed a piece of paper and wrote the message down.

It was the most profound insight I had ever written.
The experience and the message itself felt intensely charged with energy.
The energy radiated through my heart and crown chakra.
My whole body was tingling.
As the messages continued flowing through the stream of consciousness, I decided to keep writing from sunset to past midnight.
Writing and meditating was so blissful.

The next morning, a martial arts student, Kevin Dodd, came to the house for a private lesson.

The moment I opened the front door, he said,

"You look different, what have you been doing?"

Before I told Kevin what had happened, I asked him to read the first message I had received. As he was reading, it became clear that he was enjoying what he was reading and I could feel that he was in bliss. He read the rest of the messages and said "we need to put this in a booklet format."

We proceeded to create the original 25 page booklet that I shared with my family and friends in 1997. The little booklet took a life of its own. I would get letters and phone calls from family and friends, telling me how it had helped them in their own lives.

It was a humbling experience that I was grateful and thankful for.

Seventeen years later, in 2014, I began writing every day, with the intent to complete the Energetic book series that this book is part of.

I made a decision to revisit the original booklet, share the story of what happened and how it impacted my energetic way of life.

Here is the first message that I received on top of the summit.

The message was loud and clear.

"It does not have to be this way.
The warriors were and still are
an elite group of people.
They are the protectors of the land and
their loved ones.
We can all train together with
love, peace and harmony.
To love each other, is to love oneself.
By loving oneself, we love the world.
To be a warrior, is to be a scholar.
And all warriors/scholars are the true healers.
They healed themselves,
and they continue to heal the world.
The best healers in the world are
the real warriors of life.
The healer faces death on a daily basis,
looks it in the eye, and chooses life.
Life is the art of peace."

Energetic Questions & Answers

After I returned from the summit behind the house, I sat down on my sofa for the preparation to meditate again. With my eyes open, I began with the rhythmic breathing;

Energetic Breathing 3, 1, 3, 1
Inhale for 3 seconds, Hold for 1.
Exhale for 3 seconds, Hold for 1.
Repeat for 9 full cycles.
(Smile as you practice this exercise).

The moment I closed my eyes, I felt the blissful consciousness energy of
Yasū' al-Masih (Jesus, the Anointed One),
Saint Francis of Assisi and
O'Sensei Morihei Ueshiba.
The energy radiated all around my reading room, filling it with energetic light, peace and harmony.

This time, I had a pen and paper ready.
My physical/energetic life was never the same again.
More on this in the following chapters.

Note to the reader:
Digest and savour each question and answer
before moving on to the next one.
I encourage you to self reflect and see how you can apply what you are about to read in different aspects of your life........... Enjoy.

How will I know what to do?

"When the time comes.
We will know everything we need to know."

I was thinking to myself, this is so great.
I have so many life questions that I have always
wanted to ask. . . Then I asked.

I have a simple question for you.
What happens when we die?

"When we die, the physical body dies, and that's it.
Your spirit goes to the spirit world.
In the spirit world you don't need any of your
physical things like food, water, cars, etc.
In the spirit world,
the only thing you need, is your spirit.
Covering your spirit will be your custom clothing,
whatever your life on Earth is or was,
you become it.
When you live your purpose of life in your physical
world, you enter the spirit world.
By not living and fulfilling your physical journey,
you get another chance all over again.

For bonus Karmic Points, assist as many people as
you can, to fulfill their purpose in life.
Helping others to help themselves."

So, why are we here on Planet Earth?

*"Planet Earth is one of the most beautiful places
in the Universe.
It's a beginning and definitely not an end,
so live with joy.
To be joyous, is to know the meaning of life.
So, when we learn our earthly lessons while loving
and being with Mother Earth,
we need to take care of it,
just like it takes care of us.
Death is just a graduation of life
into the spirit world.
If you learned the lessons well, you enter.
If not, you get another chance.
You can have as many past lives, as you want.
Stop wishing,
what you could have been or would have been.
Begin to BE, starting now.
Live your purpose. It is stored inside of you.
You, and only you, will know.
Pray and meditate.
Ask, and you will Receive. Seek, and you Shall find.
Knock, and the door will be Open
to your Divine Heart and Soul.
The answers will come pouring out of your heart."*

How many questions can I ask?

*"If they are simple,
you can ask as many as you like."*

All right then.

Share with me the greater purpose of life.

"We love your simple questions.
The greater purpose in life is
to love one another
just the way we love you."

Okay, how do we love one another?

*"To love one another, is to forgive one another.
When you stand and pray,
forgive anything you may have against anyone,
so that your father in heaven will forgive the wrongs
you have done."*

Is it true, we have guardian angels?

"It is true!
Guardian angels are all around us,
physically and in spirit.
Your best friends and loved ones
are your physical angels.
To assist you in your purpose of life,
you have many spiritual angels that keep an eye on
you and give you a hand when you need help.
They look out for you.
When you are in harmony with your purpose of life,
you begin to see them and they will teach you
profound spiritual experiences.
Take your time, stay focused, and be joyous.
Enjoy your physical experience and
your spiritual journey."

Okay, what's up with all the fighting that's going on around the world?

"You see, fighting is an interesting illusion.
People think they have to fight,
to prove to themselves that they are right,
and that the other is wrong or not worthy.
What they are really doing,
is fighting with themselves to prove to themselves
that they can be right.
The excuse of fighting gives them permission
to live a happy life.
Somehow they get that all mixed up and forget the
purpose and the mission of the fight.
By focusing on your mission,
fighting becomes passé.
To experience life is to be
joyous, peaceful and harmonious."

What is the best way to get along with each other?

"Is to get along with each other.
Do you see what I mean?
By asking the question and already knowing,
the answer is within the question."

You are answering all my questions!

"To be able to ask a question,
you have already simplified the answer
by asking the question.
When you ask the question in your heart and soul,
the answer is waiting to be answered.
Every question you have ever asked...
You already knew the answer.
That's why you asked the question."

Is there such a thing as a Soulmate?

"Absolutely. Soulmates are all around;
males, females, plants and friends
of the animal kingdom.
You have soulmates from all aspects of
your earthly journey.
Our best friends are our Soulmates.
Have you ever met someone for the first time and it
feels like you have known them all your life?
They are your Soulmates.
Or, have you ever met someone you couldn't stand
and then they became your best friend?
They are also your Soulmates.
What you couldn't stand in them
was what you had to work on.
And when you did, they became your best friends."

So how does that work, when friends fight?

"The opposite also happens.
You meet someone for the first time, you get along.
It feels like they are your long lost friend
(which they are).
All of the sudden the two of you
don't get along anymore.
The crossroads of life is what's happening,
and it's okay.
It's more beautiful to wish each other the best of
success and to bless the friendship you have had and
will continue to have.
Whether or not you ever meet again in the physical
world. We will all meet again sooner or later."

How do we stay on our spiritual path to enlightenment?

"I love your simple questions.
Every night before going to bed,
feed your mind with spiritual thoughts.
As soon as you wake up,
feed yourself with spiritual thoughts.
Spiritual food for thoughts is very important.
Especially when you are
going to bed and waking up.
Things to avoid include watching television, surfing
the internet or reading the newspaper before going
to bed and first thing in the morning.
Ask yourself,
"What are you feeding your spiritual thoughts?"
Stay focused and be positive."

What do you eat?

"Now, all I eat is spiritual thoughts.
It's the highest form of nutrition.
When I was a physical being having an eating
experience, I ate what was put in front of me.
Then I started to listen to what my body as a whole
needed, not what my stomach craved.
Bon appetite my friend."

What do you mean by, what your stomach craved?

"Sometimes our body is craving food,
what it's really craving is water.
When we are craving potato chips what we are in
real need of, is some good sea salt to activate the
electric charge in our body.
Other times we are craving coffee for the purpose of
having more energy or to calm us down.
The reality is, we need to focus on our breath and
our thoughts to guide us through
the ups and downs of life.
As well as, how we can manage our life
more freely."

The energy in the room seemed to calm right down. Talking about food reminded me that I should drink some more water.

This is very important to do after meditating.

As I got up from my meditation to walk around,

I suddenly began to experience a tingling feeling on top of my head. It felt as though my crown chakra energy field was touching the ceiling.

After drinking some water and walking around,

I sat down and the tingling sensation went away.

As soon as I stood up, I could feel the pressure of the ceiling pressing upon my crown chakra.

I sat down to meditate again,

to allow the stream of consciousness to keep flowing.

With my eyes open, I began to practice the

Energetic Breathing 3, 1, 3, 1

Inhale for 3 seconds, Hold for 1.

Exhale for 3 seconds, Hold for 1.

Repeat for 9 full cycles.

(Smile as you practice this exercise).

Then, I tuned into the energy
and asked a few more questions.

Sex, Drugs and Rock & Roll?

"That's three questions in one.
We can only answer one question at a time.
Keep it simple, so that we can have an answer."

Okay, how about sex?

"Sex is a wonderful thing.
Your sexual energy is your creative energy,
if applied correctly with love and harmony.

If misused,
it turns into a drug of destruction and misery.

Cultivated into creativity,
it's the most profound energy available.
Sexual transmutation is
the highest form of alchemy."

All right, how about drugs?

"Drugs are a waste of time.
They derail you from your journey,
by giving you false hope of finding your journey.
That's what part of the Sixties was all about.
People wanted to get in tune by getting tuned.
Your spiritual path will lead you to the most
powerful moments you will ever experience.
No drug addiction in the world can ever come close.
Also, be aware of your everyday drug addictions
such as coffee, sugar, alcohol, tobacco smoking, etc.
Your body houses your soul.
Keep your body clean and vital, so your spirit
can continue to grow on the path of enlightenment."

Rock and Roll?

"Music is beautiful.
The key is to keep reminding yourself of the kinds of
food you are feeding your soul.
If it is positive or relaxing and upbeat music,
have fun with it and go dancing.
Music has the power to shift your emotions
and your experiences.
That's why it is used effectively in movies
to alter our mood from being sad to being happy,
in a matter of seconds.
Certain songs will trigger positive or negative
emotions, based on the experience we are
associating with the melody or the words."

Explain the oneness of love making.

"Love making is when two souls harmoniously unite
through romance, love and sex.
To become one,
to evolve as one,
to be joyous in the presence of one another.
To make love is to be in love.
When you are in love,
you are one with the universe."

Tell us more about the harmonious union.

"When a male and female come together,
they create a harmonious union of one.
Within this union there are three pillars
that create that oneness.
The pillars of romance, love and sex.
Within the three pillars there are three modalities
that are triggered in each pillar.
They are visual, auditory and kinaesthetic.
For example, within romance,
you can express it visually by giving your partner
a flower or a beautiful smile.
You can express auditory by reading them a poem,
listening to beautiful music together, or
letting them know how much you appreciate them.
You can express yourself kinaesthetically
by touching and hugging.
The same would apply to expressing yourself
through the three modalities
within the three pillars."

Almost forgot about money. . .

"Money is good.
Money is a powerful energy
that will make you more of who you are.
Money was invented as
a means of exchanging value.
Value is helping each other become more evolved.
Money helps us build houses, hospitals, roads,
libraries, schools, and so on.
Money is a beautiful lesson!
You can possess money,
or you can be possessed by money.
Crime, greed and envy
are the downfall of this illusion.
Giving, sharing and becoming are the true
transformation of money.
Befriend money. Treat it with respect.
Help others to help themselves.
Remember the great saying:
"If you give a person a fish,
you feed that person for the day.
If you teach a person how to fish,
you feed them for life." "

What's the deal with cancer, diabetes, etc.?

"Call it what you want.
There is only one dis-ease.
Dis-ease is when you are out of sync
with yourself and the universe.
To be at ease with yourself,
you become the universe.
We store negative and positive emotion
in our body.
Positive emotions empower us.
Negative emotions disable us.
By releasing the negative emotions, we learn the
lesson and continue upon our journey.
Purify and cleanse your body.
It's the temple of your soul.
Breathe fresh air regularly.
Drink clean and energized water.
Eat water rich foods.
Chew your food slowly.
Live in moderation.
Listen to your body and what it needs."

Tell us more about emotional healing!

*"Forgiveness of self and others
is the quickest way to heal your emotions.
There is one principle you will find
in every healing system around the world.
The body heals itself.
At the same time, the body can withstand poisonous
toxins, smoke and drug contamination.
"When you stand and pray,
forgive anything you may have against anyone.
So that your Father in Heaven
Will forgive the wrongs you have done.""*

Tell us about physical pain!

"Pain is a gift that nobody wants.
It's your internal fire alarm system letting you know
there is discomfort or danger ahead.
Disabling the fire alarm system and hoping the fire
will just go away, seems to be the common belief,
and temporarily relief is promoted and advocated
world-wide.
Unfortunately, the common response to pain
management of millions of people world-wide
is self-medicating with over-the-counter and
prescription drugs.
Once you acknowledge the pain
and the root cause of it,
you will be able to manage the relief in a much
quicker way than you have ever done so before.

Earlier you talked about everyday drugs and addictions. . .

"There are nine core addictions that you will witness almost every human being struggle with.

They are:

Food addiction
Sex addiction
Drug addiction
Alcohol addiction
Tobacco smoking addiction
Sugar addiction
Caffeine addiction
Gambling addiction
Drifting addiction

Addictions are a form of sabotaging your earthly journey, life's vision, purpose and mission.
Keep in mind, all addictions are self-created habits.
You had the willpower to create them,
you also have the willpower to
free yourself from them."

You already shared with us some profound thoughts about food addiction, sex addiction and drug addiction. Tell us more about the other addictions like alcohol, smoking tobacco, sugar, caffeine, gambling and drifting addiction.

Alcohol Addiction?

"Let's say a person began their alcohol addiction in high-school or college years. If they were to go back one year from the time the addiction trigger began, they would find that they had no craving for alcohol. They really needed to work hard on this habit so that it became an alcohol addiction.
There are many reasons behind the reasoning of creating this habit. For some, it may be that they have an allergic reaction to sugar and yeast.
The candida in their body is craving them to drink alcohol so that they can keep the candida alive.
The most common signs are itchy eyes, stuffy nose and skin flushing. Many First Nation (Aboriginal) cultures around the world are highly allergic to alcohol, processed sugar and yeast. Their digestive systems are not used to the processed foods they are currently consuming. Diabetes has also become an epidemic in their communities.
For others, the addiction could have started with an emotional trauma that was triggered in their childhood. They began to use alcohol to suppress and numb their painful emotions and experiences. People may love to party and celebrate. Alcohol became the vehicle for that feeling of celebration. Unfortunately, thousands of people die each year from drinking and driving, and alcohol poisoning. Keep in mind, you are an Energetic Being, having a spiritual earthly experience.

Tobacco Smoking Addiction?

"Tobacco smokers in general are very friendly and social people. They enjoy the sense of community and connection with each other.
Many believe that smoking is a way to de-stress or suppress their emotions.
Social pressure is a great negative motivator of wanting to fit in and be cool, like friends or celebrities. No one actually likes smoking when they first try it out. Being cool overrides the discomfort and then it becomes an addictive habit.
Smoking can damage every cell in the body of the smokers and those around them.
Even though we are well informed of the fact that tobacco smoking is the single greatest risk factor affecting the heart, liver and lungs, it is the #1 self-destructive habit known to humanity.
Individuals that smoke can, with some effort, convert their skill of smoking to the skill of breathing fresh air.
They have a great potential of becoming a great meditator."

Sugar Addiction?

"Sugar is an addictive poison substance that destroys every blood cell in the body.
It robs the nutritional levels and increases the probability of Alzheimer's disease, Heart disease, Diabetes, and Cancer of all kinds.

A trillion dollar food industry likes to confuse the consumers by disguising the sugar name under fructose, dextrose, fruit concentrate, corn syrup, maltose, and sucrose (table sugar).

90% of all packaged food has sugar added to it.
The average person worldwide consumes over 30 teaspoons of sugar per day,
4 grams of sugar equal 1 teaspoon.
1 Tbs of ketchup contains around 1 Tsp of sugar.
1 can of Pepsi, 7-Up, Sprite, Coco-Cola has an average of 40 grams of sugar,
which equal 10 teaspoons of sugar.
(The standard can size is 12 US fl oz or 355 ml.)

The addiction begins at a very young age, as a reward for doing something good in our childhood. Everywhere a child goes, someone is offering the child some sugar as a treat.
Parents need to start thinking of sugar treats as an addictive poison substance."

Caffeine Addiction?

"Caffeine, the trillion dollar addiction industry that keeps the world buzzing around.

With growing popularity and a marketing boom for coffee, soda drinks and caffeinated drinks, they have become the most popular social drink in the world. Caffeine is a chemically addictive substance that over 80% of adults around the world use daily. Caffeine has a mild addiction compared to alcohol, tobacco smoking and sugar.

It still takes a few weeks to get over the dreaded headaches, fatigue and nausea symptoms when you stop drinking any caffeinated drinks.

During the detoxing process, your brain will naturally cleanse the caffeine addictive substance. Once caffeine is absorbed through the small intestine, it flows into your blood stream and then it penetrates the blood-brain barrier. It enters the brain cells and creates a numbing effect, enhancing the addiction. This is why it is called the most widely used drug on the planet.

Caffeine acidifies the blood stream and causes the kidneys to release magnesium and other essential minerals into your blood stream to balance blood pH levels.

If you do not believe that you are addicted to caffeine, avoid drinking caffeinated drinks for 21 days and find out for yourself."

Gambling Addiction?

*"The thrill of winning it all and the withdrawal of
losing it all, keeps the gambling industry alive.
This drives millions of people to gamble their joy
and misery away.*
*As glamorous as Las Vegas, Reno, Atlantic City,
Monte Carlo and Macau are, their massive success
is the direct result of their customers losing millions
of dollars on a daily basis.*
*Gambling addiction is like any other addiction.
It has similar stimulus that alter the brain chemistry
to escape reality and the thrill of that winning
feeling that so many people crave because it is
lacking in their own life journey.*

*Gambling comes in many forms, whether it's casino
gambling, online gambling, lottery tickets at your
grocery store, scratch cards at the pub, sports
betting and racing, playing the stock market,
pyramid schemes, or playing bingo at your local
church or community hall.*

*Denial of any addiction is a great illusion with an
attempt to mask the pain for a better day to come.
Behind every addiction, there is pain that needs to
be healed.*

You mentioned "Drifting" as the ninth addiction, what exactly do you mean?

"Drifting is the first addiction we need to master upon our life's Energetic journey. Sometimes, it is easier to discuss the obvious physical addictions because they are easier to relate to.

Drifting is the core source of all addictions. It keeps us distracted from accomplishing our true goals and dreams.

Have you ever noticed how easy it is to distract yourself from something that is important to you?

Have you caught yourself talking on the phone for hours, then telling your friends how busy you are?

Have you been a victim of shopping for useless things to buy, only to never use?

How about surfing the internet for hours a day, and calling it research?

Other times you distract yourself with something else that is mundane and useless.

Be mindful of your drifting thoughts and activities. Allow yourself to stay focused and your spirit to align with your daily activities, focusing towards your vision, purpose and mission."

Thank You, for the wonderful and inspiring question and answer meditation that you allowed me to experience in your presence.

Energetic Listening & Seeing

Life has a unique way of guiding us toward the things we want to learn and experience. Even though sometimes it takes a few years or a decade to fully understand the lessons we needed to learn.

Almost every day, I would walk up to the summit behind the house to go for an Energetic Walk through the fields or to meditate. Other days, I would go to the summit to practice or teach the martial arts style I developed in 1989, known as Cyclone Fighting Arts.
The feelings of the energetic experience with
O'Sensei Morihei Ueshiba kept flowing through me.
The messages and lessons continued to appear at the beginning, middle or end of my energetic walk.
On one of my energetic walks, I was thinking to learn the Tai Chi Sword Form, which the old masters were able to charge and transmit energy through their body and weapons. I had read about it in "Tai Chi Classics" and really wanted to experience it. I was thinking to myself, "It would be great to find an Energetic Tai Chi teacher that can explain and teach how to move our intrinsic energy through a sword or anything we desire, to charge and transmit for the purpose of healing."
A few months went by. On another energetic walk, as I was reaching the top of the summit, I saw an older Chinese gentleman practicing the Tai Chi Sword Form.
I recognized the form immediately. My first thought was, "Is this an energetic experience that I am having, or a physical one?"

I closed my eyes and took a deep breath to calm my mind from the excitement of seeing this teacher that I wished for. There he was.

Smiling, I opened my eyes to see the older Chinese gentleman, smiling back with his beautiful welcoming eyes.

I approached him to introduce myself,

"Hello my name is Fred." While we were shaking hands, he replied with a heavy Chinese accent,

"My name is Mr Su."

I continued by saying, "Nice to meet you."

He waved his hand and responded,

"Sorry no speaking English."

We began to laugh. I asked him to please continue what he was doing. I stood back and watched his graceful movements of the Tai Chi Sword Form. In my really poor Chinese and sign language, I asked Mr Su if he would be willing to teach me the Tai Chi Sword Form.

He pointed at the sun and drew a full circle in the air. Then he tapped his watch to indicate we would meet the following day at 10:00am.

I was so excited. I headed to meet him again the next day as we had arranged.

He was not there. I was thinking, "Well, maybe we totally messed up the whole sign language exchange that we had yesterday."

Thirty minutes later, Mr Su arrived and seemed very apologetic. Attempting to explain why he was late, we both started laughing and moved on with the planned class.

Mr Su had a very unique and progressive way of teaching. He would start slowly by demonstrating the first section of the form. Then he had me watch it from different locations so that I would get a different perspective from all directions.

We then did the first section of the form together a few times. Then he asked me to practice by myself, and gracefully corrected every move I would make.

He brought to my attention the importance of breathing while moving at the same time to cultivate the intrinsic energy into ones center and how we can transmit the energy from our center, through our body, to and through the sword.

We met regularly. Either one or two sun circles in the air would indicate our next lesson.

A few sun circles later, in the middle of the class, we saw a Chinese lady with her children walking by us, smiling as she watched. Mr. Su and I looked at each other and smiled. We were thinking the same thing, "We have someone that can translate for us."

I approached the lady and asked her if she would be willing to translate from English to Chinese. She said she would, as long as he spoke the same dialect. She spoke Cantonese and luckily, Mr. Su spoke Mandarin and Cantonese.

I was so happy I could ask Mr. Su some questions and he could fully understand what I was saying and freely express his teachings.

Mr Su was a retired professor from a University in Beijing. He was visiting his son in Victoria, BC, where his son taught at the local university.

I was very lucky to train with Mr Su during his summer holidays in Canada before he headed back to Beijing, China.

I began to really appreciate how life has a unique way of putting the right teachers and lessons right in front of us, at the right time, upon our life's journey. It's up to us to seize the moment and learn as the opportunity presents itself.

In the past, I had many similar experiences when meeting my martial arts, energetic healing arts teachers and mentors. They all seemed to appear when I was ready to study with them and they were willing to teach me.

After this experience, I had a new appreciation for how **Energetic Thoughts** are transformed into reality.

One day, I was walking around downtown headed to a Japanese restaurant. I felt that someone I knew was walking beside me.
It was a familiar energy that I was sensing and feeling.
I looked around but no-one there looked familiar.
As I continued to walk, I felt the same presence again.
I looked to my left and my right, nothing here or there.

I stopped for a moment to take a deep breath and saw Professor Al Carty, my teacher and good friend that was looking back at me.

Realizing that we were both heading to the same restaurant, we started to laugh.

With a smile he said, "What took you so long?"

I nodded my head in agreement.

We walked into the restaurant to have lunch.

Our conversations were almost always about martial arts and energetic healing arts. This time, Professor Carty was sharing with me the principles of

Traditional Chinese Medicine and how, and why the energetic meridians played a major role in Martial Arts and the Healing Arts. All these subjects I had studied and researched independently, until he reminded me that, "They are one and the same, it's all about our perception and intention."

A simple concept that would have a profound impact on my martial arts and energetic healing arts.

A few weeks later Professor Carty called me at home to ask a few questions about my Clairvoyant ability, wondering why I was hiding this energetic ability.

In his loving and direct way, he said,
"I know you can see the energetic aura and the chakras. It is your natural ability. Why are you hiding what you see?"

This was a hard question for me to answer, so I quickly changed the subject.

Since my childhood, I had the ability to see energetically. It used to freak me out because I never knew how to make sense of it as a child. I dealt with it as best as I could throughout my life.

Not letting go of the subject I was trying to avoid, Professor Carty said, "You and I know you can see energetically. Now tell me, what you are seeing?"

I proceeded to tell him what I was seeing around his energetic body over the telephone. His feedback was very encouraging, and lead me to more experimentation which continued for a few years.

The more I opened up to the energetic listening and seeing, the more lessons appeared flowing through me and from me on a daily basis.
I began to journal all my insights, inspirations and lessons I had learnt from all my teachers.

Allow me to quickly introduce my martial arts and energetic healing teachers in the order of meeting them. A more detailed list of my teachers, including the lessons and stories of how I met them will be in future books from this Energetic book series.

In the meantime,
Coach Kurt Hufetlein: Boxing Coach
Sensei Chris Fournie: Kickboxing and Arnis
Grandmaster Remy A. Presas: Modern Arnis
Datu Shishir Inocalla: Modern Arnis & Hilot
Datu Kelly S. Worden: Natural Spirit Way
Sufi James A. Keating: Comtech
Professor Bob Anderson: Executive Protection
Sensei David John Harris: Yeung Chuan
Grandmaster Bobby Taboada: Balintawak
Professor Al Carty: Pressure Points
Grandmaster Fook Yueng: Chi Kung
Professor Jesse Glover: Non-Classical Gung Fu
Grandmaster Choa Kok Sui: Pranic Healing
Master Nona Castro: Crystal Healing
Master Fe Pacheco: Clairaudience
Master Gregory Castanarez: Clairvoyance
Professor Su: Tai Chi Sword Form
Maestro Sonny Umpad: Visayan Escrima
Dr. Stewart Blaikie : Body Alignment and Structure.

When you meet a real master of the arts, their lessons come in waves. On the day you met them, then days and weeks after, then years later you reflect back on how they impacted what you do and how you do it.

It's important to have a balance of external and internal forms of insight and learning.

My internal learning and meditation took a new direction of energetic seeing and listening to the messages flowing through the stream of consciousness of life.

I began to pay more attention to the ability of listening to the deep insight that my Divine Soul wanted to share with my physical consciousness.

Before any meditation, I always begin with,

Energetic Breathing; 3, 1, 3, 1
Inhale for 3 seconds, Hold for 1.
Exhale for 3 seconds, Hold for 1.
Repeat for 9 cycles.
(Smile as you practice this exercise).

After the rhythmic energetic breathing, I would fully relax my whole body and allow my thoughts to clear my conscious awareness and enter the space of nothingness were all things are created.

Then, I would tune into the energy of my Divine Soul and I would simply listen to the message of the day. Each day, I received an appropriate message that would guide me through the day, week, month or the year. Some days, I would receive ideas for books, nutritional insights, martial arts principles and other days, I would just continue the blissful meditation into what became the New Moon Meditation CD in 1998.

Some of the messages were as simple as practicing the "Colour Of The Day" or listening and tuning into the nothingness between the everyday human made noise. You will be surprised to find that silent moments in nature are rare. There is always some car, train, boat or a plane going by. You have to go deep into the woods to hear "The Pure Sounds of Nothingness".

This exercises will be explored in the following chapter, 21 Day Challenge.

The energetic messages continued to flow on a daily basis. I began to think in different ways that I had never thought of. Things I was taught to believe are true until I found out that there are many layers of truth.

Guiding me to shift my paradigm and perception.

The teachings came through in different ways.

Some were based on conversations, ideas, passages, parables, movies, books, studying nature, emotions, behaviours, physical structure, as well as, the constant thought that,

"We are Energetic Beings having a physical experience at the same time."

One very thought provoking lesson I learned through Energetic Messages, assisted me in many ways. "Remember what you forgot, and forget what you need to remember".

Boom, the lights went on.

In an instant, transformation occurred. I was fully empowered and energized. I began to remember what I had always known deep in my heart.

I re-remembered all the things I had forgotten to remember, and forgot all the things I needed to remember. So deep and profound that night when I went to sleep. I had many vivid dreams of my past, present and future life. I began to discover skills and talents that I never knew I had in the past or could discover in the near future.

The teachings, the lessons, the experiences, all came alive. The next day when I woke up, all the things I needed to remember to do were mysteriously forgotten. Things I had to do and needed to do, were not the things I wanted to do. From that day on, I became really aware of my time and commitments to myself, and others.

Allow me now to share with you the 21 Day Challenge, that I practice and apply to every aspect of my life. These lessons came through and from Energetic Messages that I received and sequenced.

I highly encourage you to fully participate in experiencing the 21 Day Challenge.

Energetic Questions: 21 Day Challenge

Disclaimer: Before starting any positive challenge that may alter your life forever,
make sure you check in with the doctor within.

Welcome to the 21 Day Challenge that will positively impact your life forever.

Since 1989, I have been teaching martial arts and personal empowerment workshops to thousands of people from around the world. The ones that truly succeeded, were the ones that participated in a 21 Day Challenge of some form to create a new empowering habit which they wanted to develop and master. All of the advanced martial arts students and individuals that I personally coached and mentored, have reported back to me with some amazing results. I am also excited to hear back from you and your success stories from the 21 Day Challenge you are about to experience.

"Our self-image and our habits tend to go together.
Change one and you will automatically
change the other." Maxwell Maltz

One of my favourite authors, Maxwell Maltz wrote extensively in his well known book Psycho-Cyberntics, about the importance of creating a new positive habit. He states numerous times throughout his books, that it takes a minimum of 21 days to develop a habit or to create a new self-image.

Keep in mind that, he stated, a "minimum."

21 Days is a great foundational start to create a new habit and self-image. In our advanced martial arts training we apply the same principles to 90 days to fully embody the new habit, skill and self-image.

My goal for this sequence of lessons is to create a momentum of empowering energetic habits that will positively impact your daily life.

I would like to invite you to fully participate in each lesson every day for the next 21 days.

As you go through each lesson, be mindful of the previous lessons. As you move ahead into the future lesson, you will notice a nice momentum from one lesson to the other. You will embody the teachings in a whole new way of learning, thinking and living.

Each 7 days are connected. For this reason, I highly encourage you to actually follow the given sequence for achieving maximum results.

You will find that I added extra pages called "Insights, Inspirations & Ideas," on the left side to most lessons. Feel free to be creative and write all over this book.
Turn this section of the book into your own journal.

Signature of Commitment

Make a commitment to yourself, that you will participate and complete the 21 Day Challenge.

I have tested the below method in my workshops and coaching sessions, with great results.

The starting day can be any time you desire, and the best time to start is right now.

Your signature of commitment creates an energetic connection of alignment towards completing your
21 Day Challenge:

Starting Date: _____

Signature: _____

Witness: _____

I highly recommend you to repeat the 21 Day Challenge, one month from today.

Starting Date: _____

Signature: _____

Witness: _____

Insights, Inspirations & Ideas

-

-

-

-

-

-

-

-

-

Day 1: Colour of the Day

This is a great lesson to enhance our visual awareness and perception. For this lesson to be effective, you will need to answer the questions as you are reading this page. Avoid skimming through the lesson before answering each question.

What is your favourite colour?
Your answer is:
For best results pick one of the below colours.
Primary Colours: Red, Yellow or Blue.
Complementary Colours: Green, Purple or Orange.

Let's say you choose "Red".
Look around the room you are in.
How many red objects do you see?
You may have answered 5 or 10.

Take a deep breath. Calm your mind and take a look again, as if you were looking for the very first time. See how many red objects you can really see. There is a great chance that the number of red objects doubled.

How does this happen?
We are deletion creatures. We see what we need to see and we delete the rest.

For this week, pick your favourite colour and go through the day looking for that colour. You will be amazed at what you will discover.

Insights, Inspirations & Ideas

-
-
-
-
-
-
-
-

Day 2: Energetic Breathing 3, 1, 3, 1

Breathing is the single most important aspect of human survival. Yet, few people know how to rhythmically breathe correctly. Shortness of breath is a major challenge for many people that are experiencing different forms of physical and mental dis-ease. This simple exercise can potentially help bring your health, fitness and well-being into ease.

Take a moment to observe your breathing pattern.
Do you inhale through your nose or mouth?
Do you exhale through your nose or mouth?
Do you hold your breath after you inhale or exhale?

Energetic Breathing; 3, 1, 3, 1
Inhale for 3 seconds, Hold for 1.
Exhale for 3 seconds, Hold for 1.
Repeat for 9 cycles.
(Smile as you practice this exercise).

Inhale through your nose for 3 seconds all the way to your energy center. This is located roughly two fingers below the navel, two fingers deep.
Hold for 1 second and smile.
Exhale through your mouth for 3 seconds.
Hold for 1 second and smile.
Practise for 9 cycles, a total of 72 seconds.
Repeat every hour, on the hour. It takes 12 minutes to practice this 10 cycles, throughout the day.

Insights, Inspirations & Ideas

-

-

-

-

-

-

-

-

-

Day 3: Energetic Center

Our Energetic Center is located roughly two fingers below the navel, and two fingers deep.

It is also known as DanTian in Traditional Chinese Medicine, Chi Kung and Tai Chi. In Japanese, it is called Hara. In Pranic Healing, it is referred to as Secondary Navel Chakra. In anatomy, it is called Center of Gravity. Our Energetic Center allows us to create a balance between our spiritual, mental, emotional and physical bodies.

I once asked my teacher, Grand Master Choa Kok Sui, the founder of Pranic Healing, "What's it like to be in your center all of the time?" He replied saying, "I am not in my center all of the time. I am just able to connect with my center very quickly when I need to."

Different challenges come our way on a daily basis. The key to mastering any situation, is to learn how to quickly return to our center.

For some people, it takes a day, a week, a month or years to return to their center when they are mad or angry at someone. By returning your focus of breath to your center in 10 seconds or less, you are on your way to mastery. You see this with all masterful professional athletes. When someone irritates them while they are playing their game, they have the ability to recover much quicker than the average player.

Practice the Energetic Breathing 3, 1, 3, 1 into your Energetic Center as you go through your day.

Day 4 : Inner Compass

Have you ever wanted to make a decision about something to do or not to do, and dwelled on it for days and weeks? We all have.

This simple exercise checks and balances your physical and energetic alignment before making any major decisions.

Today, you will discover which way you lean when you are out of balance and how to adjust your inner compass bearing. Inner Compass is our inner guide to knowing, balancing and deciding by utilizing our whole body. Inner Compass will positively impact the way you walk, talk, and stand in life.

If you do not have a physical compass, you can download one to your mobile phone, or make one at home using a needle and cork.

Refer to the illustration:

Facing Magnetic North. Stand with your feet parallel to each other, hip width apart and pointing forward. As you stand tall, close your eyes and notice which way your body might be swaying, leaning or being pulled towards. Make a mental note of this direction. Open your eyes and gently move three times back and forth between this and the opposite direction.

Gently move your body back and forth, in each of the eight main directions of the compass
(N to S, E to W, NW to SE and NE to SW).

Stand in neutral position and practice the Energetic Breathing 3, 1, 3, 1 for three cycles.

Day 5: Sit, Stand or Wobble

There is an ancient esoteric teaching that states,
"When you stand, Stand. When you sit, Sit.
In the middle be aware of Wobbling."

In between sitting and standing is the moment of truth,
where many individuals experience wobbling.
Wobbling is an unstable equilibrium feeling that will
reflect in our physical, emotional, mental and spiritual
life. Here is a balancing body alignment exercise that
you can practice at home, or at the office. It will allow
you to trigger the correct kinetic alignment of your
major joints.

Refer to the illustration:

Use a firm seat that will allow you to align your body as
follows: thighs parallel to the ground, forming a right
angle with your lower legs, as well as, your back. Have
your knees and feet hip width apart. Your head should
naturally be an extension of your spine, forming a
vertical line between your ear and shoulder when seen
from the side.
You will find that the correct seat hight will be essential
for the right angle alignment. Sitting towards the edge of
your seat may make the transitions easier. Take care to
sit back correctly on the seat.
With your feet parallel to each other and pointing
forward, practice both ways of standing up and sitting
back down as illustrated.

Day 6: Aligning, Grounding & Rooting

Aligning is the ability to allow the Energetic Divine to flow through us and from us at all times, guiding us to become spiritually aligned in our physical realm. The energy enters through our crown chakra, (crown halo) through the spine to activate all the minor and major chakras (meridians) as the electric circuit roots the energy through our foot chakras and the base spine energy grounds us into the Earth.

We will use the 3 prong plug and outlet as a metaphor to explain the electrical/energetic connection between aligning, rooting and grounding. The right terminal is "live" (Right Foot Chakra), the left terminal is "neutral" (Left Foot Chakra), and the bottom terminal is "ground" (Base Spine Chakra). The electricity flow through the "live terminal" and powers your device. Then it flows into the "neutral terminal" to complete the circuit. The purpose of the "ground terminal," is a safety feature that turns off the breaker to avoid potential electric shock (Kundalini syndrome).

Refer to the illustration:

Stand with your feet parallel, hip width apart.
Begin the Energetic Breathing 3, 1, 3, 1
Allow the energy to flow through your whole body.
Then visualize the foot chakra rooting you into the Earth, like a tree and a beam of light flowing from your spine, grounding you into the Earth.
Remain aware of aligning, grounding and rooting throughout the day.

Insights, Inspirations & Ideas

-

-

-

-

-

-

-

-

-

Day 7: Energetic Walking

Energetic Walking is the process of utilizing everything we have learned so far. The enhancement of our visual perception of our surroundings with, *Colour of the Day, Energetic Breathing 3, 1, 3, 1,* awareness of our *Energetic Center,* aligning ourself with our *Inner Compass,* the practice of *Sit, Stand or Wobble* and *Aligning, Grounding & Rooting.*

Now, let's apply all of the above lessons while we go for a walk in a natural environment.

Energetic Walking for 20 to 30 minutes a day can greatly improve our overall health and well-being. While studying Nutritional Microscopy (Live and Dried Blood Analysis), I gained a new appreciation for the Lymphatic System and how it works. The lymphatic system does not have a pump and the best natural way to activate it, and enjoy the many benefits it has to offer, is through walking. Many great thinkers of our time have been avid walkers for inspirations and ideas also.

As you go for a walk, make sure your hands and shoulders are free of any bags, purses, or other objects. If at all possible, avoid your mobile phone.
Walk with your feet parallel, hip width apart.
Your head and all major joints should be relaxed and free flowing. Make sure you smile as you walk freely and effortlessly throughout the day.
You should feel energized after your walk.

Day 8: Pure Sounds of Nothingness

"Now and again, it is necessary to seclude yourself among deep mountains and hidden valleys to restore your link to the source of life."
O'Sensei Morihei Ueshiba

Pure Sounds of Nothingness is a musical orchestra of the Earth, speaking to our core essence.

If you live in the city, it's next to impossible to experience the Pure Sounds of Nothingness for longer than a few minutes. In the middle of the night, you will find that there is much artificial noise pollution in every town and city around the world. Even in remote locations, there is always some car, train, boat, or plane going by. When you can hear yourself walk in nature, that is a good location to explore. See if you can go on a hike or a remote beach to experience this magical earthly connection.

One exercise I would encourage you to do is, attempt to audiotape all natural sounds only for 20 minutes. It may seem like an easy task to achieve. You have to be honest with yourself; you really have to listen to the natural sounds of your location, and the artificial noise interruptions. As soon as you hear any artificial noise, you have to start taping again. It took me a few weeks of changing locations, to capture 20 minutes of Pure Sound of Nothingness.

Once you find that magical spot, visit it on a daily, weekly or monthly basis to practice your energetic walking, breathing, meditating and creative journaling.

Day 9: Plateau into Momentum

Congratulations, keep the momentum flowing all the way till the end of the 21 Day Challenge.

Momentum is a progression of movements that are created just like an ocean wave.

You can become part of the flow of momentum, be caught by the wave, and ride it to create the momentum that you desire in any aspect of your life. My Energetic Martial Arts teacher, Sensei David John Harris always shared with me the importance of taking some action daily towards a desired goal.

"If you feel that you are at a plateau, you can continue your level of progression by reading a book on the subject, watching a video or by attending a seminar or you can mentally rehearse your desired goal or outcome. It is important to do something, regardless of how small or how large."

Think of something you are currently working on, in your personal or professional life, where you feel like you hit a plateau.

Determine where you are right now and where you want to go, or what you would like to accomplish.

Begin right now, with a small step towards your desired outcome. Once you break through the plateau, you begin to appreciate momentum at a whole new level.

Apply this to different aspects of your life.

Insights, Inspirations & Ideas

-

-

-

-

-

-

-

-

Day 10: Hemisphere Alignment

This is a great physical, mental and energetic exercise. Through my coaching and mentoring program, I have seen it help numerous individuals that were experiencing confusion, dizziness, and wobbling. Once the equilibrium between the left and right hemisphere are in sync with each other, a whole life alignment begins to take place.

While coaching certain individuals, I noticed that some were able to jump into a new habit very easily and effortlessly. While others had many challenges committing to a daily ritual.

Early development of the right and left hemisphere alignment begins with crawling, walking and running. Unfortunately, modern limited daily movement creates many body dysfunctions, that lead to lifelong dis- abilities. I began to use specific martial arts exercises, along with body alignment movements that help to trigger the right and the left hemispheres alignment of any individual.

A simple assessment that you can do by yourself to discover your right and left habitual patterns:
Notice which leg you use when putting on your pants, socks and shoes. After you have determined which sequence you are using, I would like you to reverse the sequence for one week. Also, notice your dominant ear that you use when talking on the phone. Just for fun, try switching sides and see how your concentration and attention span are affected.

Enjoy the process of alignment.

Insights, Inspirations & Ideas

-

-

-

-

-

-

-

-

-

Day 11: Energetic Gratefulness

My long time Firewalking friend Brian Ludwig came for a visit. During our conversation, he noticed that, I was having a bad day. I was complaining about this and that. He simply smiled and said, "Let me ask you a question, a question that you like to ask the participants at your Firewalking Seminars."

"What are you Grateful for in your Life?"

Instantly, my attitude changed. I began to share what I was grateful for in my life. I affectionally call Brian, the "Avalanche Man," because he literally survived a snow avalanche while working in a copper mine in Northern Canada. (Read Brian's inspiring story on my website).

This personal experience inspired me to interview many happy, healthy and wealthy people. They all seem to have one common attribute, the sense of gratefulness about every aspect of their lives. Whenever I had the opportunity to go for a walk with them, they all had a sense of gratitude for nature and people.

Allow me to ask you the same 5 Grateful Questions that I ask myself every morning when I wake up.

What are you Grateful for that makes you Happy?
What are you Grateful for in your Health?
What are you Grateful for in your Wealth?
What are you Grateful for in your Life?
What are you Grateful for right Now?

Insights, Inspirations & Ideas

-

-

-

-

-

-

-

-

-

Day 12: Energetic Greatness

We can become, achieve, awaken and transform anything our heart desires, along the path of our life's calling. I truly believe that every living person has an inborn talent that is waiting to be expressed into energetic greatness.

Every skill, strategy and habit has a unique energy frequency. Once we understand and connect to the correct energetic vibrational frequency of our physical, emotional, mental and spiritual realm, our lives will be transformed in ways we never thought possible.

I would like to share with you how to discover or rediscover your multi-dimensional skills of greatness. Once you have mastered one skill, you can master many.

There is a common saying that limits people and boxes them in: "A jack of all trades, master of none."
I would like to dispute this saying by stating that, the person who coined this may have known only one skill. You are a multi-dimensional diamond.

1. Write down all skills of greatness you have ever been good at.

2. Go through your list and discover the common thread that ties all your skills together.

3. Which of these skills would you like to master?

In the next lesson we will explore more questions to get you closer to your Energetic Greatness.

Insights, Inspirations & Ideas

-

-

-

-

-

-

-

-

-

Day 13: Vision, Purpose and Mission

When your vision, purpose and mission are clear, your greatness will appear in everything you do.

Take a moment to answer these three simple, yet very thought provoking questions.

Write what you can right now.

Then tomorrow, revisit this page before moving on to the next lesson.

Take your time to enhance your answer, as many times as you want until it resonates in your heart.

What is your vision in life?

What is your purpose in life?

What is your mission in life?

Insights, Inspirations & Ideas

-

-

-

-

-

-

-

-

-

Day 14: Mutual Mentoring

In the book, Think and Grow Rich by Napoleon Hill, he shares the importance of the mastermind principles, mutual association and mentoring towards a common goal. I have used these principles throughout my life to align with specific friends that have similar aspirations and skills.

I'd like to impress upon you, the importance of aligning yourself with individuals who you can openly share your vision, purpose and mission, and for whom you can do the same. Be aware of sharing your vision, purpose and mission with individuals who have no interest in your success.

You have to be very selective when choosing your mutual mentor. You can waste many years with the incorrect energy match that can derail you from your goal and desired outcome.

Many of my firewalking and martial arts students have become my mentors in their chosen expertise. My good friend and long time Cyclone Fighting Arts Blackbelt, Jesse Knotts helped me understand and appreciate the game of golf. He enthusiastically improved my golf swing and putting skills. He has become a body dynamic expert in both, the field of golf and martial arts.

Think of a skill you would like to learn that one of your friends is an expert at. Then, consider what you can offer them in return.

For mutual mentoring and the friendship to continue, it has to be a win/win/win exchange.

Insights, Inspirations & Ideas

-

-

-

-

-

-

-

-

-

Day 15: Energetic Thoughts

We are constantly transmitting Energetic Thoughts at different frequencies throughout the day, much like radio stations do. We also have the ability to receive thousands of radio frequencies from around the world. As we tune into these radio frequencies and choose to listen to one specific song, we are actually tuning into the energetic vibrational frequency of that song. We can be happy, sad, joyful or excited. We may sing along or hum the tune for a few minutes, or even all day. If we are not in harmony with the song we are listening to, we can either complain about the song or we can simply change channels to find another song that is more in tune with our state of being and consciousness.

We use the same Energetic Thoughts to be positive or negative. By thinking happy, peaceful, and joyful thoughts, our lives will be blessed with happiness, health and wealth. We have all experienced the phenomenon of thinking of someone and that someone calls us on the phone, emails us or we see them walking down the street. This is a wonderful confirmation of energetic thoughts, transmitting through the airwaves.

Something to think about!

What Energetic Thought are you transmitting through the airwaves?

What Energetic Thoughts are you receiving through the airwaves?

Day 16: Author of Your Life

Here comes one of my favourite questions that I like to ask the participants of my mentoring program.
You really have to think about this question before responding.

Who is the author of your life?

If you replied, "I am," I challenge you to dig deeper and you will find some inner wisdom waiting to be explored.
We are the fabric of our environment, behaviour, capabilities, beliefs, values, identity and spirituality.
We are influenced by our families, babysitters, friends and teachers at school, music and movie stars, authors and spiritual teachers and our community as a whole.

My friend Linda Marie Romeril is the author of a colourful collection of books for children, the first in the series being, "Rainbow the Clown."
Linda likes to remind children and parents of the magic and wonder of being who they truly are and to discover the beauty of each day.
Linda is a great example as the author of her life by living her passion for writing children stories.

Write a list of all the people, books and movies that have influenced your life in one way or another.
You will find a common thread that weaves between them all.

Insights, Inspirations & Ideas

-

-

-

-

-

-

-

-

-

Day 17: Adversity into Triumph

We have all experienced adversities of some form.
We basically have two choices, we can keep dwelling on them as a victim or we can move forward and turn an adversity into our triumph.
The news media weekly highlights stories about fallen superstars, be it a musician, actor, politician, athlete, or religious figure, fallen from grace. There is always some kind of pain that needs healing for the addiction to be transformed into triumph.
Refer to the nine core addictions that were mentioned earlier in this book.

A long time friend and Cyclone Fighting Arts Blackbelt, Nick Marinos, had a rough life growing up on a Native Reserve in Canada. His teenage years lead him to being in a street gang and all the crimes that came with it. He had a pivoting point in his life that you are able to watch in a documentary available on my website. You can also do an internet search, Tricky Nick Marinos Gladiators and Gridiron. Here is his motivation affirmation, that kept Nick focused to become a Mixed Martial Arts Welterweight Champion, Stuntman, Actor and an Author.

"I want to prove to myself and my family that I can change for the better and accomplish something great for my family and community."

Take some time today to create your own motivating affirmation. One that can transform your adversity into your triumph.

Insights, Inspirations & Ideas

-

-

-

-

-

-

-

-

-

Day 18: Energetic Blessings

Here is one of the powerful Energetic Blessings that allows you to open to the transformation of higher vibration and forgiveness.
It is taught in Eastern Esoteric Christianity and practiced on a daily basis, the parable of Mark 11:22 - 11:26

"May the Energetic Divine be within you.
I say to you, whoever shall say to this mountain:
Be lifted up and fall into the sea
and will not doubt in their heart but shall believe
that thing which they say,
anything that they say shall be done for them.
Therefore I say to you,
that everything that you pray and ask for,
believe that you are receiving it
and it shall be given to you.
And whenever you stand to pray,
forgive whatever you have against anyone,
so that the Energetic Divine will bless and
forgive the wrongs you have done."

If this parable resonates with you, read it twice a day, once upon waking and once before going to bed. You can also practice it as prayer in your meditations.

Blessings to you my friend.

Insights, Inspirations & Ideas

-

-

-

-

-

-

-

-

-

Day 19: Give to Live & Open to Receive

It is in giving that we receive and it is in receiving that we are able to give. Giving and receiving is the cycle of life, you can't have one without the other.
Opening to the possibility to receive, will give us the opportunity to give. With the ability to give, there is the opportunity to receive.

"They give that they may live, for to withhold is to perish" Gibran Khalil Gibran

Sometimes we fear opening to receive, because of previous negative experiences of people giving us something and expecting something in return. This is also known as, giving with strings attached.

We need to open our front and back heart chakra to allow the energy of giving and receiving to become one. This will allow genuine gifts to flow to us and from us, freely.

Lessons for the day:

Give and open to receive genuine compliments.
Smile as you acknowledge the divinity of the people you meet in person or talk to on the telephone with.
Give freely to someone you love and care for.
Give freely to someone you do not even know.
Acknowledge the gifts you receive today.

Insights, Inspirations & Ideas

-

-

-

-

-

-

-

-

-

Day 20: Energetic Synchronicity

We have all encountered some form of energetic synchronicity. The term synchronicity was coined by the famous Swiss, Dr. Carl Gustav Jung.
"Synchronicity is an ever present reality for those who have eyes to see."

Would you like to access the power of energetic synchronicity on a daily basis?
By acknowledging our energetic synchronicity experiences, we begin to have them on a daily basis. No matter how simple they are, we need to acknowledge them.

Write down as many energetic synchronicity experiences as you can remember, as well as, how they impacted your life.

Memory jogger for today's lesson:
You are thinking of someone and they call.
You visualize a parking spot and it's there.
You are late for a bus, train, plane or ferry and it is still waiting for you to board.
You lose your wallet and some wonderful person finds it, and returns it back to you.
You are walking in nature and you feel the presence of someone that is significant in your life.

Begin to pay attention to what you were thinking when these energetic synchronicity experiences occurred and how they made you feel.

Insights, Inspirations & Ideas

-
-
-
-
-
-
-
-
-

Day 21: Have a Beautiful Day

As a celebration of completing the 21 Day Challenge, you deserve to have a beautiful day, every single day.

Find a comfortable seat and begin this visualization with Energetic Breathing 3, 1, 3, 1 into your center.
Continue breathing throughout this exercise.
Recall a beautiful day you recently experienced. You can do this with your eyes open or closed.
Take a moment to notice what you are seeing, hearing, feeling, smelling and tasting.
As you remember this beautiful day in detail, you will notice that all your senses are engaged.
Stand up to walk around your surroundings and continue to experience this beautiful day.

Here are some things you can do to create more beautiful days in your everyday life:

Look at your favourite pictures or scenery.
Listen to your favourite music and sounds.
Experience meditating with the sunrise and sunset.
Smell your favourite flower, herbs and nature.
Taste and enjoy your favourite healthy food.
Go for a nature walk with a friend and use as many lessons from the 21 Day Challenge, as you can.

Have a Beautiful Day.
Until we meet again.

Insights, Inspirations & Ideas Action Plan
9 Things I am committed to implementing right now:

1.

2.

3.

4.

5.

6.

7.

8.

9.

Note to the Reader

If you enjoyed Energetic Questions, and you would like to share it with family, friends and associates, feel free to contact us for special rates on bulk orders.

We would also like to hear how the insights, inspirations and ideas that you gathered through this book, have helped you in your personal and business life.

For more information on Fred's Coaching and Mentoring Programs, Retreats and to receive our newsletter, please visit our website.

www.FredShadian.com
info@FredShadian.com

Energetic Questions
2 Day Retreat

You are personally invited to participate in the
Energetic Questions 2 Day Retreat,
taught by Fred Shadian.

If you liked this book, you will love this Retreat.
As a gratitude for purchasing Energetic Questions,
Life's Simple Answers, Fred Shadian is offering the
Energetic Questions 2 Day Retreat to you and a family
member to attend as his complimentary guests. This
Retreat is held in the Southern Gulf Islands, BC, Canada.

Come and experience the embodiment of the teachings
that we discussed in this book and explore the
Energetic Questions 21 Day Challenge in detail.

This 2 Day Retreat is Valued at $500.00.
This is a limited time offer valid till December 31st 2015.

To activate your complimentary ticket, please visit our
website for registration and more detailed information.

www.FredShadian.com
info@FredShadian.com

About Fred Shadian

Fred Shadian is a multi-talented researcher and student of life. He is a Coach and Mentor in Martial Arts, Firewalking, Energetic Body Alignment, Kayaking and Nutritional Microscopy.

Fred's speaking, training and healing abilities have guided thousands of individuals worldwide, including Canada, USA, Mexico, Hawaii, Ecuador, Columbia, Jordan, Lebanon, France, United Kingdom, Norway and Germany, how to achieve optimal health and discover their Energetic Greatness.

Fred and his wife Ruth live in the Southern Gulf Islands, BC, Canada. Fred has been involved in the Health and Wellness Industry for over two decades. He has appeared on BCTV, Chek TV, Canada A.M. and CBC Radio. Fred holds three BlackBelts in three different Martial Arts styles and has been teaching professionally since 1989, when he founded Cyclone Fighting Arts.

He has produced three martial arts videos, the New Moon Meditation CD and is the author of the Energetic Book series.

www.FredShadian.com
info@FredShadian.com